Made in United States
Orlando, FL
08 June 2025

61936951R00065